EXTREME COLORING
Mandalas

BARRON'S

Welcome to the world of extreme coloring – an opportunity to enjoy a relaxing pastime, develop your creativity and produce impressive works of art. All you need is a set of pens or pencils, some time to yourself and a willingness to take on a creative challenge.

This might be the first time you've tried coloring since childhood or perhaps you're an experienced color-inner with an appetite for more. Whichever category you fall into, you're in for a treat with *Extreme Coloring Mandalas*.

"Mandala" is a name given to geometric designs based on circular forms, and throughout the ages and across the world, different cultures have assigned symbolic and spiritual meanings to these beautiful patterns.

These mandalas are elaborate and intricate, but they can be colored as simply as you choose. There are no rules – it's up to you to choose how you want your mandala to look. For many, the concentration and creative decisions required provide a welcome distraction from the stresses of daily life.

So take your pens or pencils and create some beauty of your own. You'll soon be on the way to creating your own awesome, mesmerizing patterns.

"Mandala" means "wheel" or "circle" in Sanskrit, an ancient Indian language. Over thousands of years, the word has been connected with many spiritual, cultural, and decorative meanings.

The mandala is one of the oldest symbols in the history of human civilization. The Incas built their cities so that they radiated outward from a center, while early North American tribes embodied their entire cosmology in a sunwheel mandala.

The perfect circle of the mandala is reflected all across the natural world, from the sun and moon to the pristine design of a snowflake and the nucleus of an atom.

Remember, there are no rules! There is no right and wrong when coloring your mandala. It is completely up to you to decide which colors or blocks of color go where.

The circle is a meaningful symbol in many religions, cultures, and philosophies: it signifies never-ending or eternal, but equally it can embody a completeness or unity.

Mandalas are often drawn and viewed from the center of the circle outward. Try increasing the darkness or intensity – or the lightness or tint – of your colors as you work toward the circumference.

As a decorative device, the mandala has been used by everyone – from the Moors in their mosques to the Art Nouveau artists, and from the Native Americans to the Celts of Europe.

A mandala can be produced in many different ways. Some are constructed on the ground, using sand or colored grains of rice, while others are engraved, painted on walls and floors. Of course, in modern times, they are produced digitally.

Geometric patterns were introduced to Europe through the Islamic architecture and decorations of the Moors. By using turquoises, blues, greens, and reds, you can create a Moorish feel to your mandala.

Even though it may be dominated by other shapes, a mandala has a concentric structure. You may want your colors to retain the symmetry of the mandala, creating an effect of unity and harmony.

Relax! Coloring is time well spent. Many adults are in danger of forgetting how to play. As George Bernard Shaw said, "We don't stop playing because we grow old; we grow old because we stop playing."

Coloring is a form of play that enables us
to forget the demands of daily life. It can
help develop spontaneity, stimulate the
imagination, and sometimes calm the mind
in the midst of a stressful situation.

Remember to take time to look at your mandala once it's complete. Losing oneself in the beauty, symmetry, and color of the design is a key function of the mandala as an aid to meditation.

In Buddhism, the mandala is rich with symbolism and sacred meaning. At the heart of Buddhist teaching is the Wheel of Life mandala, encompassing the philosophy of a cycle of life, death, rebirth, and suffering.

To give your mandala a mystic Eastern feel,
try using a palette of colors from your
spice rack – from cinnamon brown to the
ochre of coriander, and from the pale tan
of ginger to turmeric yellow.

Sand mandalas are a feature of Tibetan Buddhism. Monks draw the geometric patterns which are filled in with colored sands. You can recreate these beautiful pieces by setting blocks of vivid colors against each other.

The design and colors of the mandala
are intended to absorb the mind and
block out distracting thoughts. By enabling
the busy mind to relax, the creative spirit
is encouraged to run free.

While some believe the colors of the rainbow
have spiritual power, others simply love
the effect of the multi-colored lines. Try
your own arrangements of red, orange,
yellow, green, blue, indigo, and violet.

The artists of the Art Nouveau period utilized mandala themes, using colors that became known as "greenery-yallery." Pick out some mustard, sage green, olive green, brown, and even gold!

Aztec mandalas were used as both calendars and spiritual expression. You could map out the colors of your year using their bright yellows, reds, and blues interspaced with blocks of black.

By coloring, you are making decisions about color choices and concentrating on hand-eye coordination. This focus can help stimulate brain areas related to motor skills, creativity, and the five senses.

"Through their symbolical content, [mandalas] exert a retroactive influence on the unconscious. They therefore possess a 'magical' significance, like icons, whose possible efficacy was never consciously felt by the patient." Psychiatrist Carl Jung.

Swiss psychiatrist Carl Jung introduced
the mandala to psychotherapy sessions. He
believed that if we are allowed to choose the
colors instinctively, it will help reveal the
unconscious forces that lie deep within us.

Try choosing your colors and patterns
instinctively. Be strict and give yourself just
seconds to select a pen and a space to color.
What, if anything, does the result reveal
about your state of mind?

For a change, try using the colors you believe you don't like. Used together, they might provide a clarity of thought – or you might even see them in a new light.

Looking for a serene mandala? For many, the patterns, rhythms, and colors of the sea inspire a sense of peace. Using blues, greens, and grays in your palette can generate a calming effect.

Remember the fabulous patterns created
by the kaleidoscopes of your childhood?
Try filling your mandala with a multitude
of colors to recreate one of the fragmented,
beautiful images produced by this toy.

The mandala is one of the most powerful
American Indian symbols. Often decorated
with furs and feathers, it can be found
on both the Plains Indian dance shields
and their medicine wheels.

Color symbolism varied from tribe to tribe, but the Native Americans would generally use earthy reds, greens, and yellows divided by thin lines of black. Try adding the sparkle of their turquoise or emerald jewelry.

Remember that your mandala is a means of capturing your attention. Create interesting patterns and devices, such as sudden explosions of striking accent colors – fluorescent pinks, purples, oranges – that will really pop.

Match your palette to your mood. If you're in
a contemplative frame of mind, head for the
blues and greens. Feeling buoyant? Then hit
the reds, oranges, and yellows with gusto!

The mandala's influence in Europe is demonstrated by the beautiful stained glass rose windows of the great cathedrals, such as the Chartres Cathedral or Notre Dame in Paris.

Create your own rose window mandala. Think of the outlines for the shapes within your mandala as the lead, then imagine the light illuminating the amber, lime green, navy blue, and violet colors.

Some think of the mandala as a means
of reflecting on the journey through the
seasons of the year. Work your way around
the circle, giving your own interpretation
of the colors of each season.

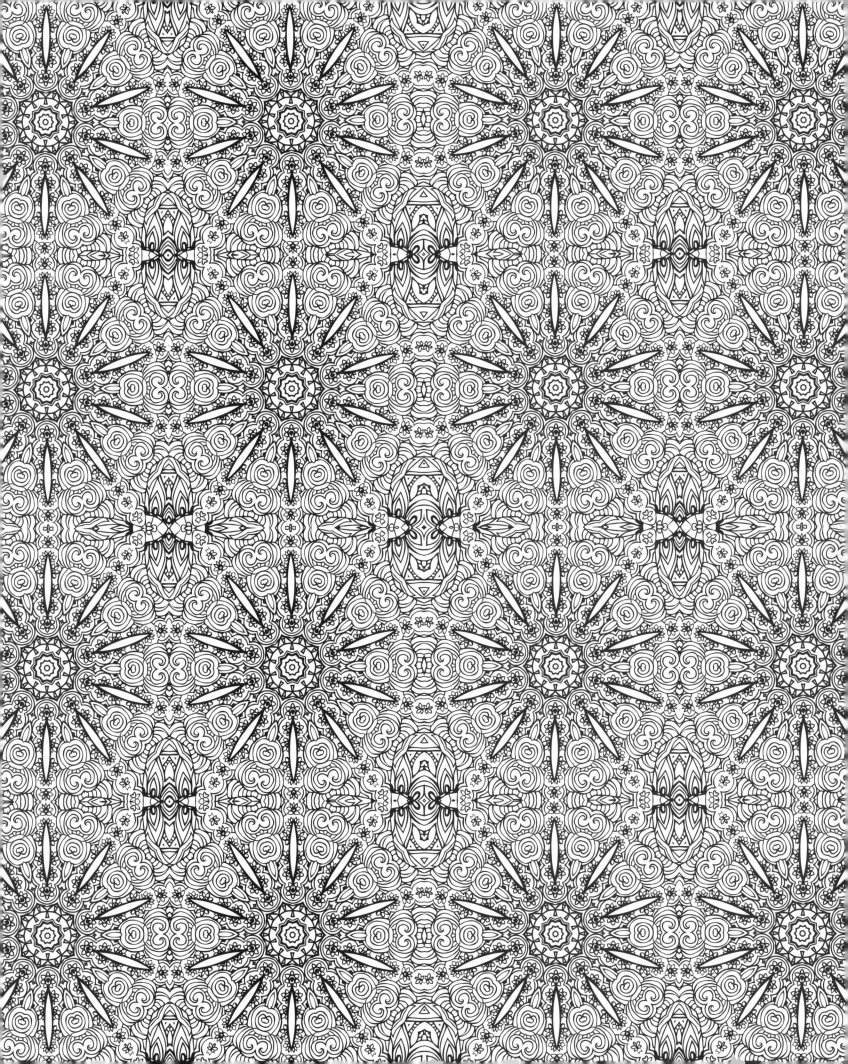

Look for the "Flower of Life" motif, a symbol of creation, among the mandalas in this book. Composed of multiple, evenly spaced, overlapping circles, they form a hexagonal flower-like pattern.

The butterfly is often an inspiration for mandalas. Its beauty, delicate nature and transformation lend it a symbolic power. Look to the colors of the Red Admiral, Purple Emperor, or the Monarch Butterfly to fill your picture.

Want to create a striking mandala? Go for it! You could try for a psychedelic effect by juxtaposing yellows, purples, and pinks, or use neon and electric colors for a punk effect.

By combining the splendor and beauty of
flowers with the mathematical magnificence of
geometrical figures, mandalas illuminate how the
natural world and the man-made world
both contrast and complement each other.

Some mandalas are considered to be symbols of sacred geometry, said to contain ancient, religious values. Patterns often follow the Fibonacci sequence or the Golden Ratio – the mathematical figures which appear across nature.

Don't forget you can color a monochrome
mandala, too. Black and white, the colors
of yin and yang, reflect the balance
of the mandala. It can look pretty
impressive on the page as well.

Monochrome doesn't have to be black and white. It can work just as well with any color and white or any two contrasting colors, particularly if you use shades of those colors. This can have real impact.

The respected psychologist David
Fontana believes mandalas can help us to
"access progressively deeper levels of the
unconscious, ultimately assisting
the meditator to experience a
mystical sense of oneness."

Mandalas have often been painted as frescoes for the walls of temples and monasteries. You can create a unique piece of art for your own walls. Consider the colors and shades of the room when selecting your palate.

The mandala is an ideal tool for relaxation or meditation. The circle directs your focus inward and the intricate geometric patterns draw your concentration. Use your colors to help lead your gaze along perpetual routes.

The mandala is a central and highly symbolic icon of Celtic artwork. Patterns of harmony and balance and dark and light are woven through them, reflecting their belief in the continuity of life and the interconnection of all things.

Mandalas are works of sacred art in
Tibetan Buddhism. Its "manual,"
The Mahavairochana-Sutra, states that
the center of the mandala should be
colored white, followed by circles of
red, yellow, blue, and black.

First edition for North America published in 2016 by Barron's Educational Series, Inc.

© Copyright 2015 by Carlton Publishing Group.

All inquiries should be addressed to:

Barron's Educational Series, Inc.
250 Wireless Boulevard,
Hauppauge, New York 11788
www.barronseduc.com

ISBN: 978-1-4380-0834-9

Manufactured by: Marquis, Louiseville, Canada

Printed in Canada

9 8 7 6 5 4

For best results, colored pencils are recommended.